Kansas

ABC Coloring Book

An ABC Learning Activity Book all about Kansas
With Count-to-10 Coloring Bonus!

Little Red Hills

Written & designed by: Rianna M. Hill

www.WyomingisHome.com

**Wyoming Is Home is a Brand of
Little Red Hills LLC**

©2023

My ABCs Kansas Coloring Book

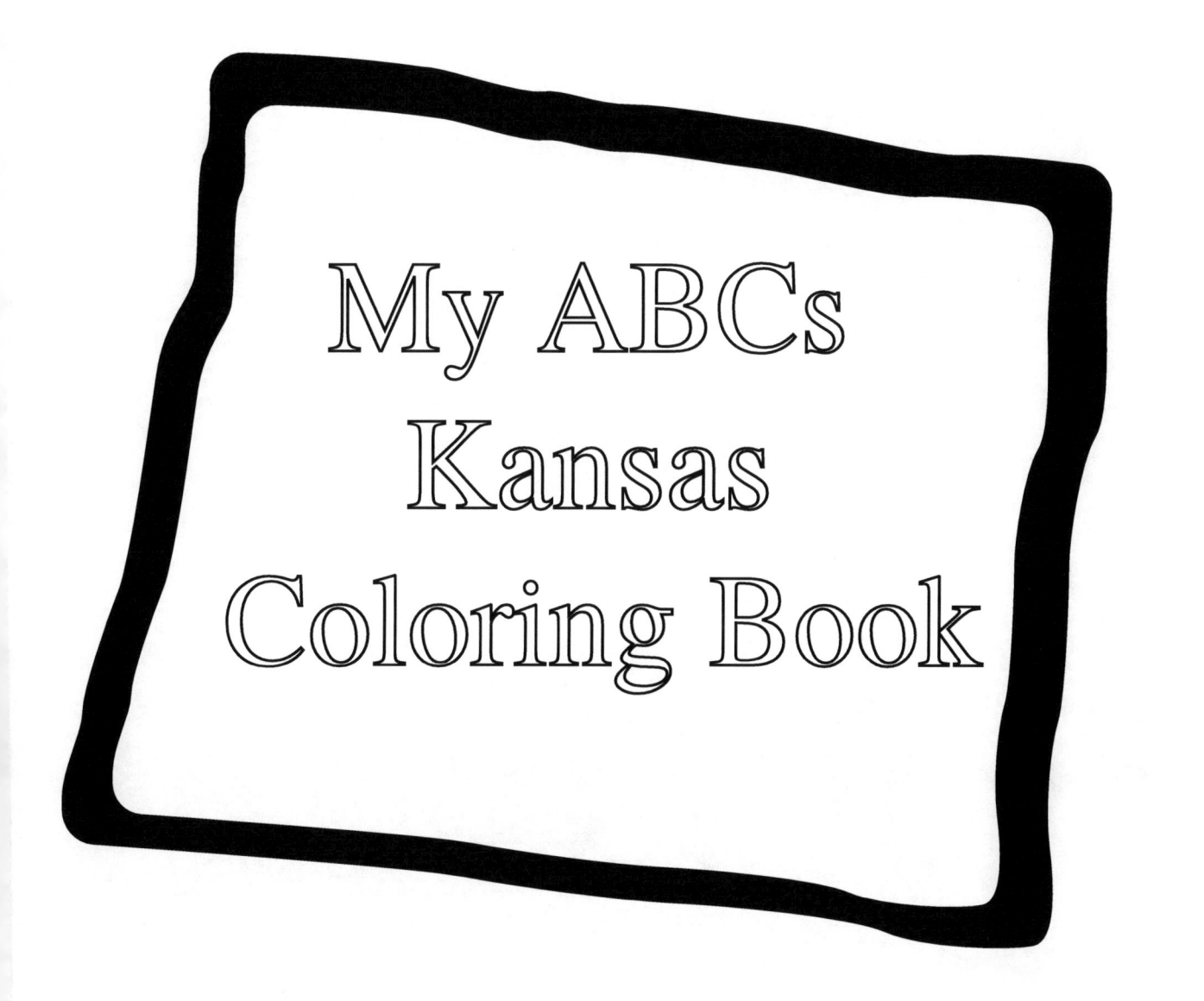

name:

A Aircraft

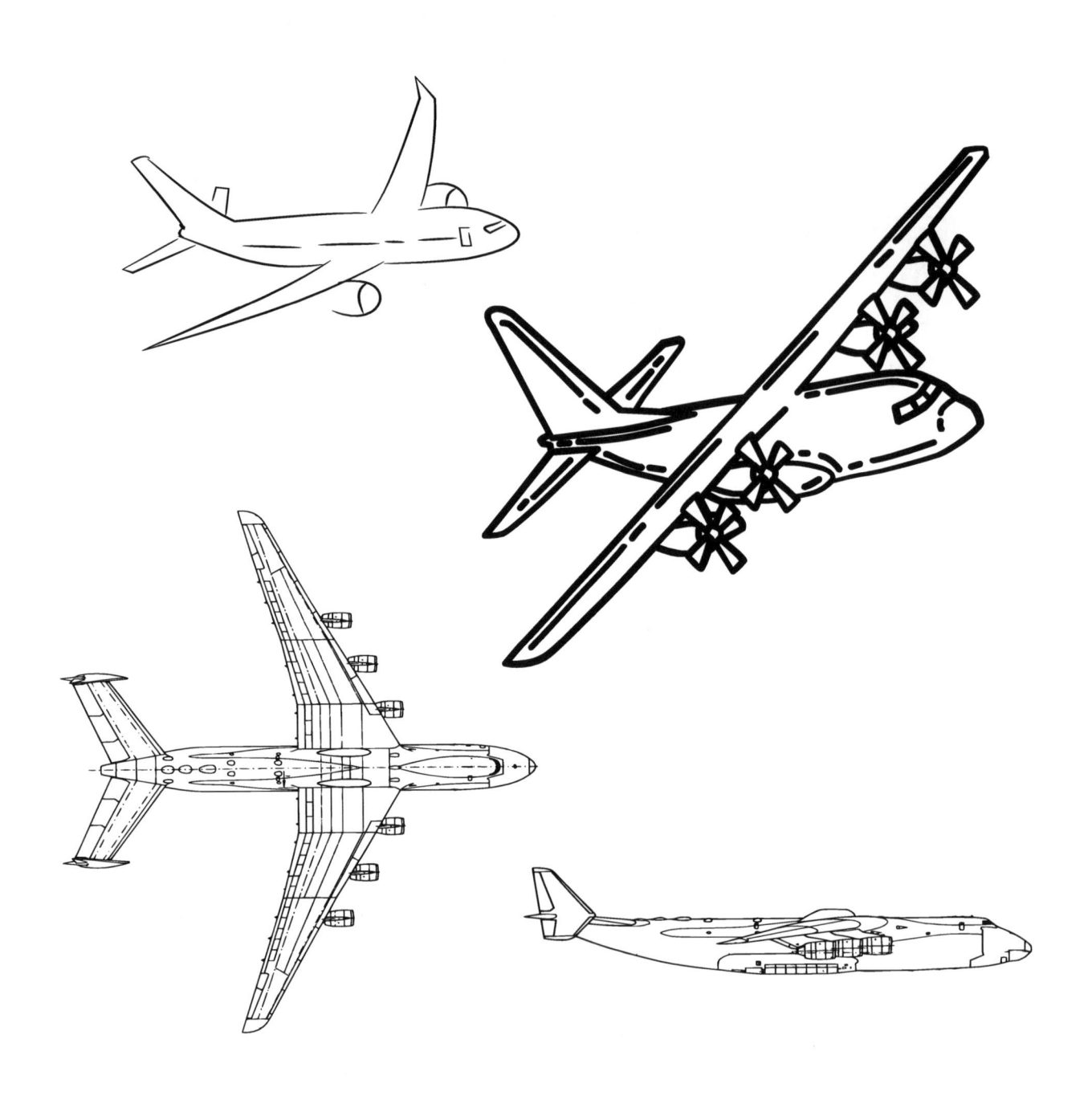

There are several aircraft factories in Kansas that have contributed significantly to the aerospace industry.

B Ball of Twine

The world's largest ball of twine is located in Cawker City, Kansas. It is approximately 41.5 feet in circumference.

C Chocolate

Russell Stover was born in Kansas in 1888. He founded the Russell Stover candy company, well known for chocolate

D

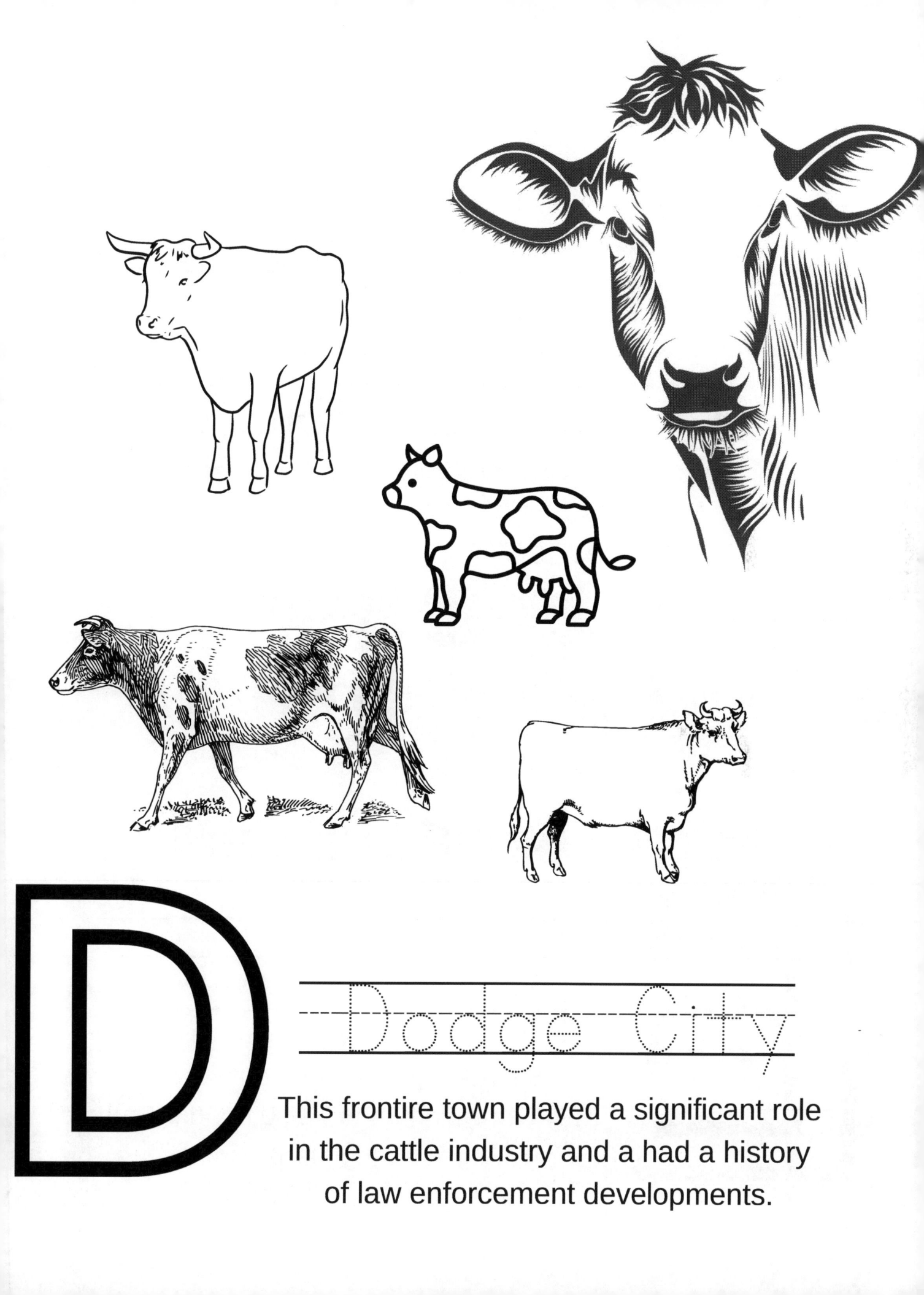

Dodge City

This frontire town played a significant role in the cattle industry and a had a history of law enforcement developments.

E   Elk

Elk are a popular big game animal in Kansas. They can weigh up to 1,000 pounds and are known for their large antlers.

F Fox

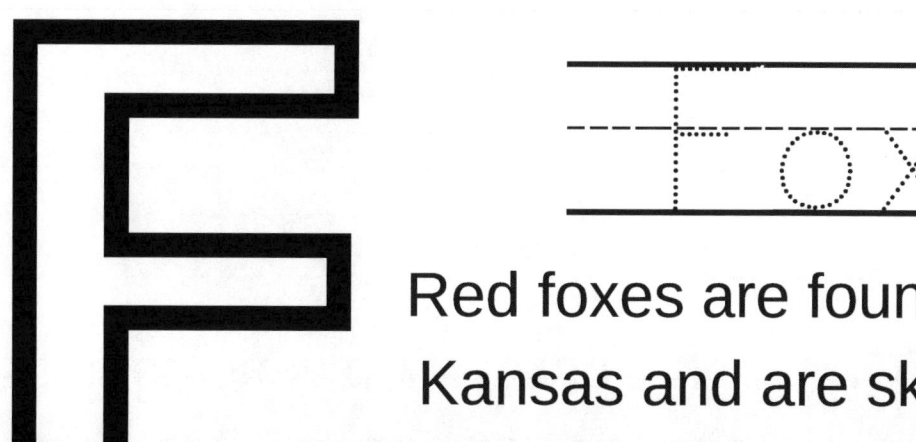

Red foxes are found throughout Kansas and are skilled hunters known for their reddish-orange fur and bushy tail.

G

Garter Snake

Garter snakes are non venomous and are common in Kansas. They are usually found in grasslands, woodlands, and wetlands.

H Hawks

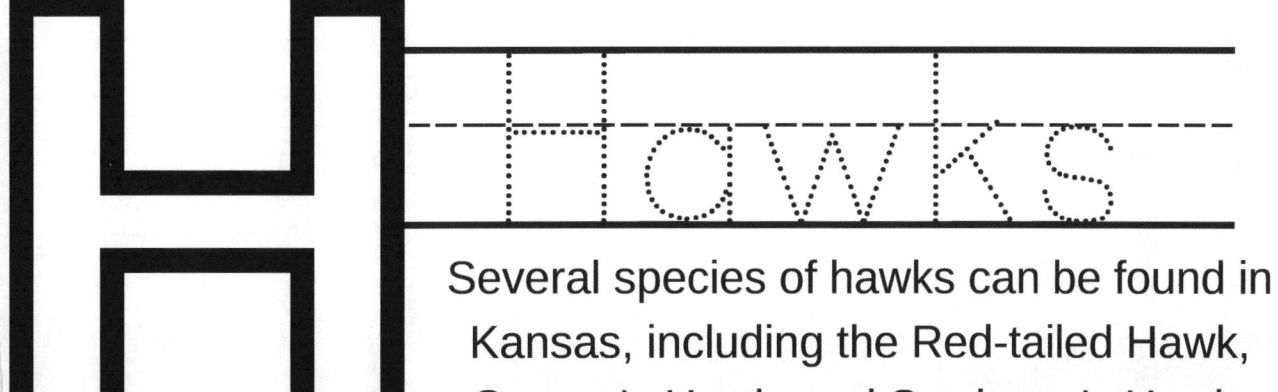

Several species of hawks can be found in Kansas, including the Red-tailed Hawk, Cooper's Hawk, and Swainson's Hawk. These birds of prey are great huntres and have great eyesight.

I

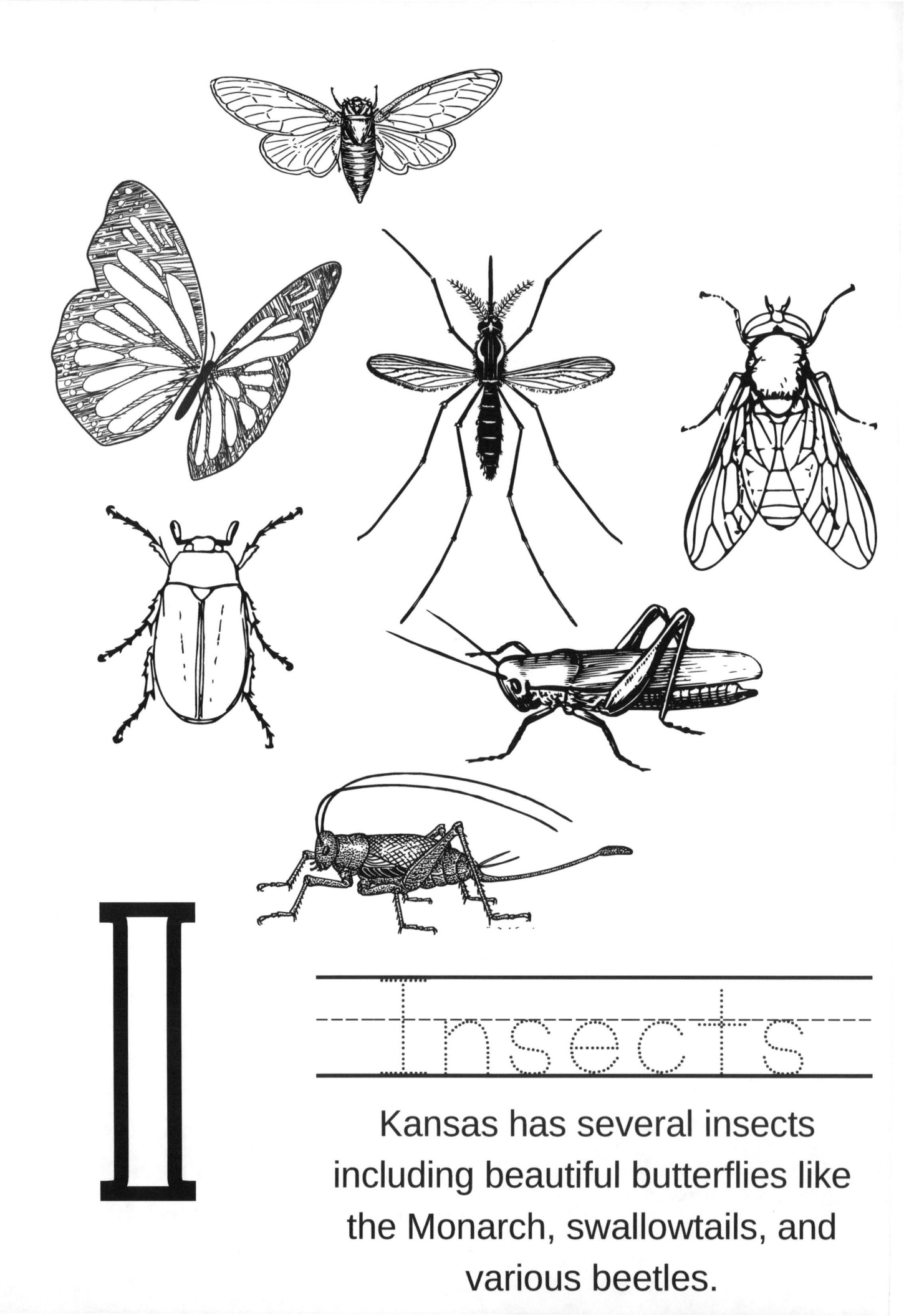

Insects

Kansas has several insects including beautiful butterflies like the Monarch, swallowtails, and various beetles.

J

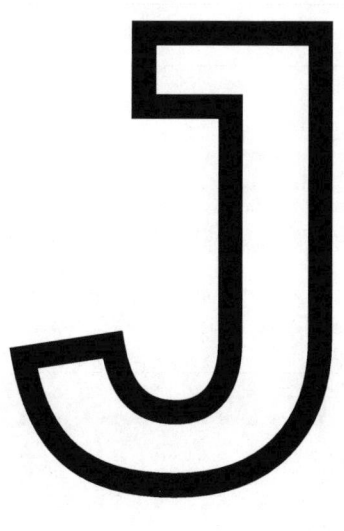

Jaybird

The Blue Jay is often referred to as the jaybird. It is a vibrant blue and white bird found in various habitats in Kansas.

K Kaw River

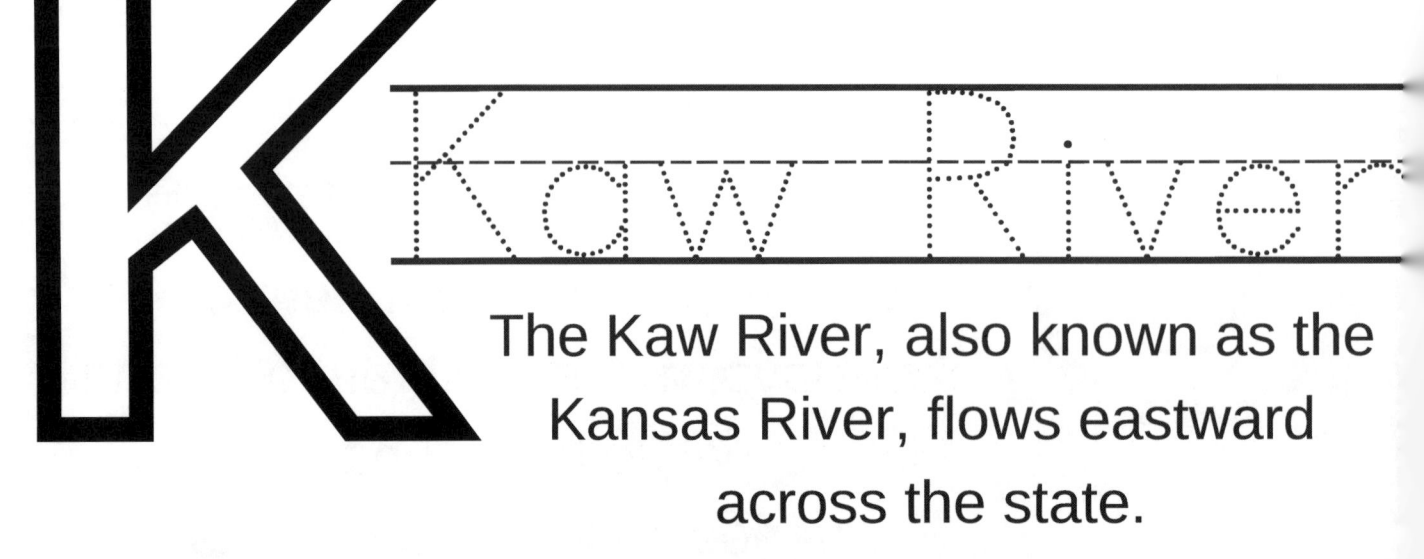

The Kaw River, also known as the Kansas River, flows eastward across the state.

Landscape

Kansas landscapes range from expansive prairies and rolling hills in the Flint Hills region, to agricultural lands, and rivers around the state.

M

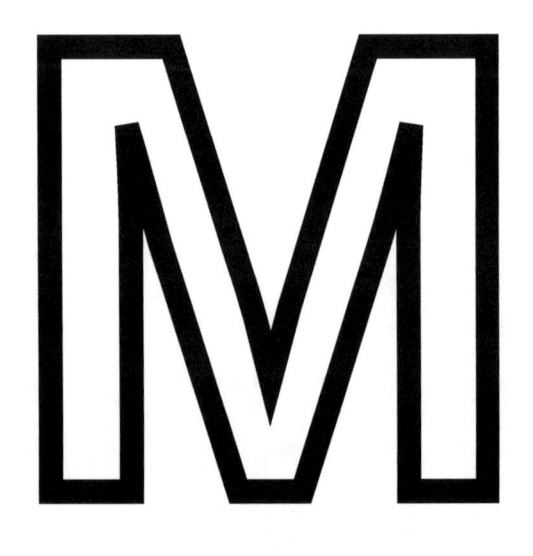

Mount Sunflower

The highest point in Kansas at 4,039 feet. It takes 14 minutes to climb the trail from the parking lot.

N

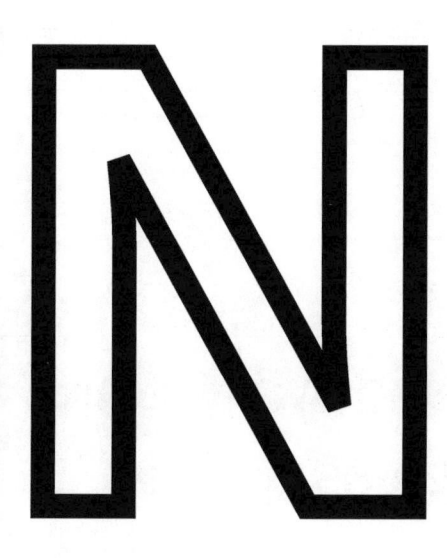

Newton

Newton is a city in Kansas known for its railroad history and the annual Chisholm Trail Festival.

O

Oak Trees

Various species of oak trees, such as the Bur Oak and White Oak, can be found across Kansas.

Pheasant

Ringneck pheasnets are the most common, orignially from Asia. They live in grasslands and prefer bushy areas.

Q

Quail

The bobwhite quail is native to Kansas and can be found in grasslands, brushy areas, and agricultural lands throughout the state. They have a very distinctive call.

RINGNECK
Ranch, Inc.

Ringneck

Ranch

R

Ringneck Ranch is a premium pheasant hunting operation in Tipton, Kansas with luxury accommodations with some of the best bird dogs in the state.

S

Sunflower

The sunflower is the state flower of Kansas designated in 1903. The tallest sunflower on record was over 30 feet tall.

T Topeka

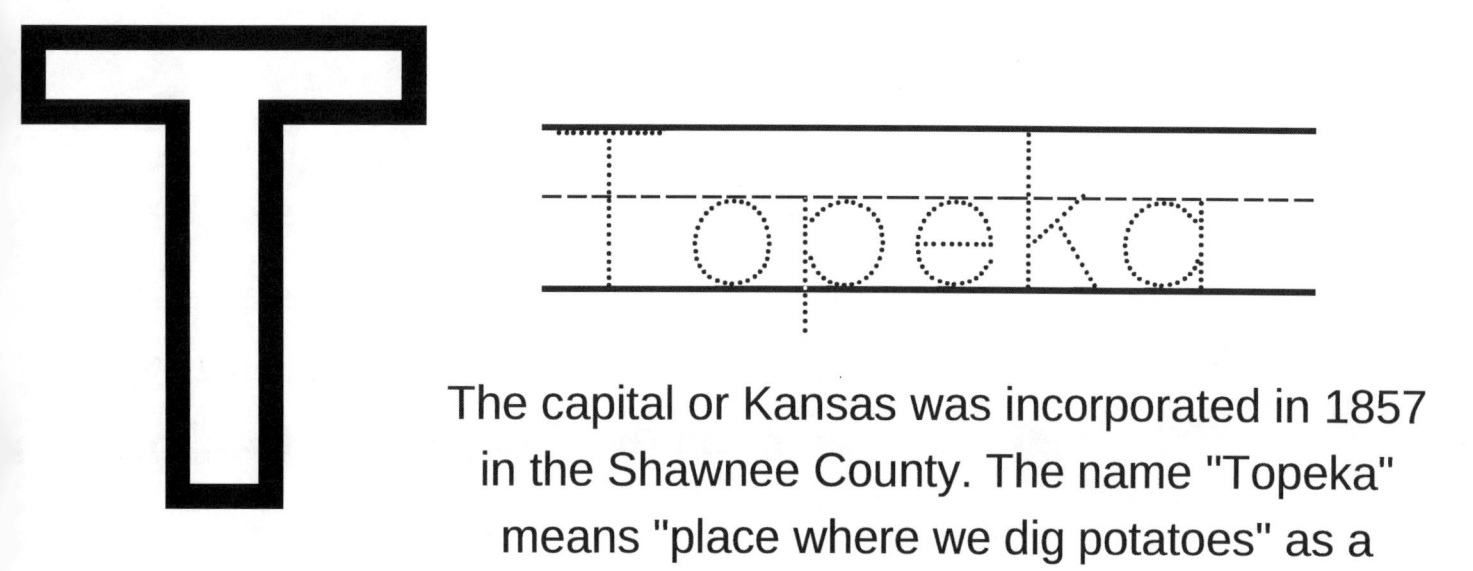

The capital or Kansas was incorporated in 1857 in the Shawnee County. The name "Topeka" means "place where we dig potatoes" as a Kansa-Osage word.

U underground salt

Kansas has many underground salt deposits, particularly in the central and western parts of the state.

V Veteran Memorials

Mant places in Kansas have dedicated memorials to honor military veterans, showcasing the state's respect and gratitude for those who have served in the armed forces.

W Wheat

Kansas produces a significant amount of wheat every year, including over 6 millio acres of winter wheat harvested in 2022

X

Xeric

"Xeric" refers to an environment characterized by dry conditions or low water availability. This is a common envirotment in Kansas.

Y

Yellow-Bellied Marmots

Yellow-bellied marmots are large ground squirrels known for their burrowing habits.

Z

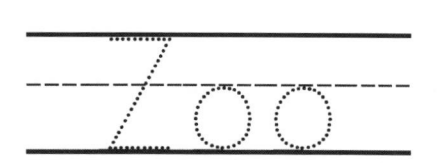

Zoo

There are 13 Zoo's in the state of Kansas, notably the zoo in Wichita has over 2,500 different species of animals.

MY COUNT TO 10 KANSAS COLORING BOOK

name:

1

one bison

2

two meadowlarks

3

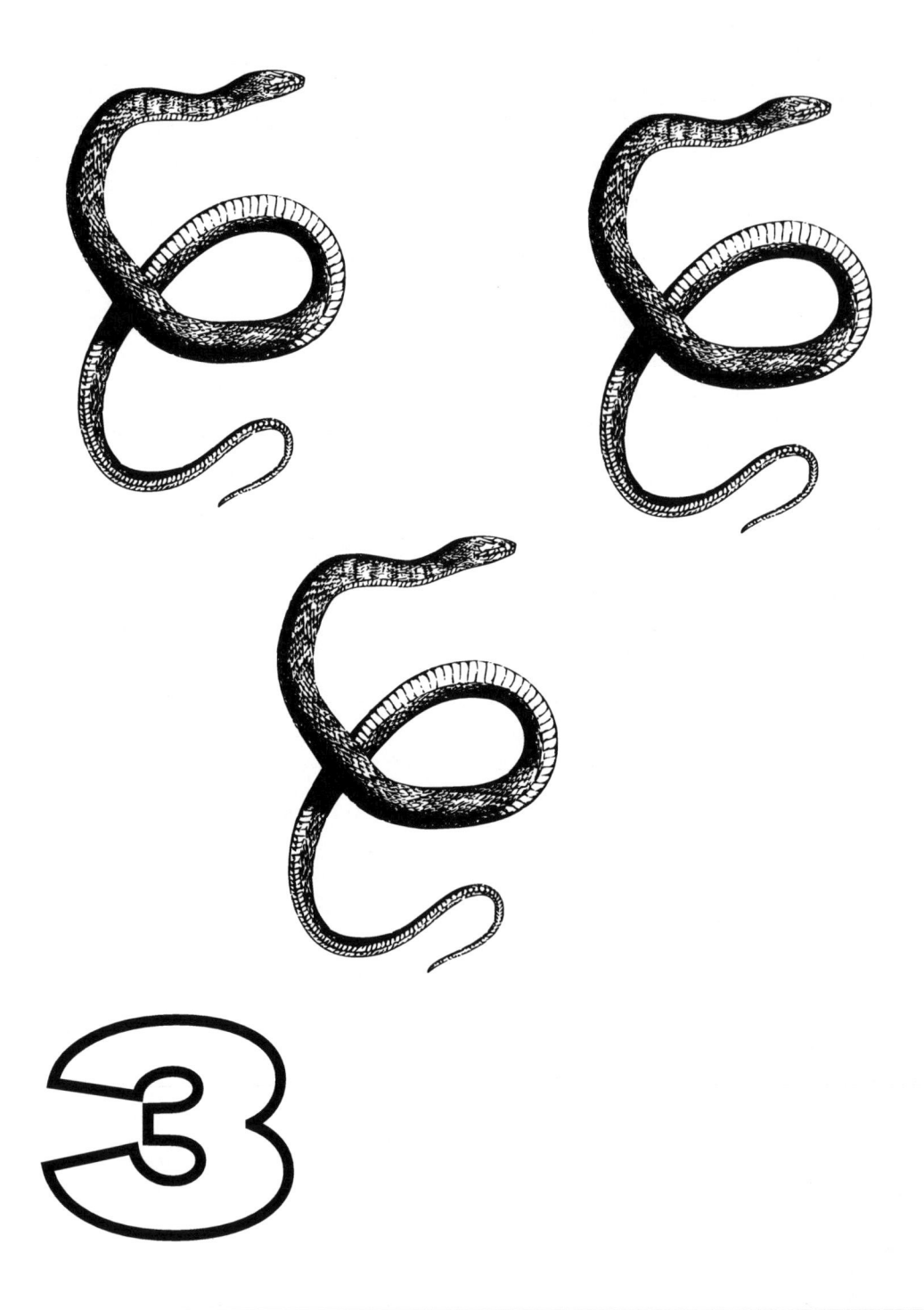

three snakes

4

four quail

5

five cows

6

six horses

7

seven elk

8

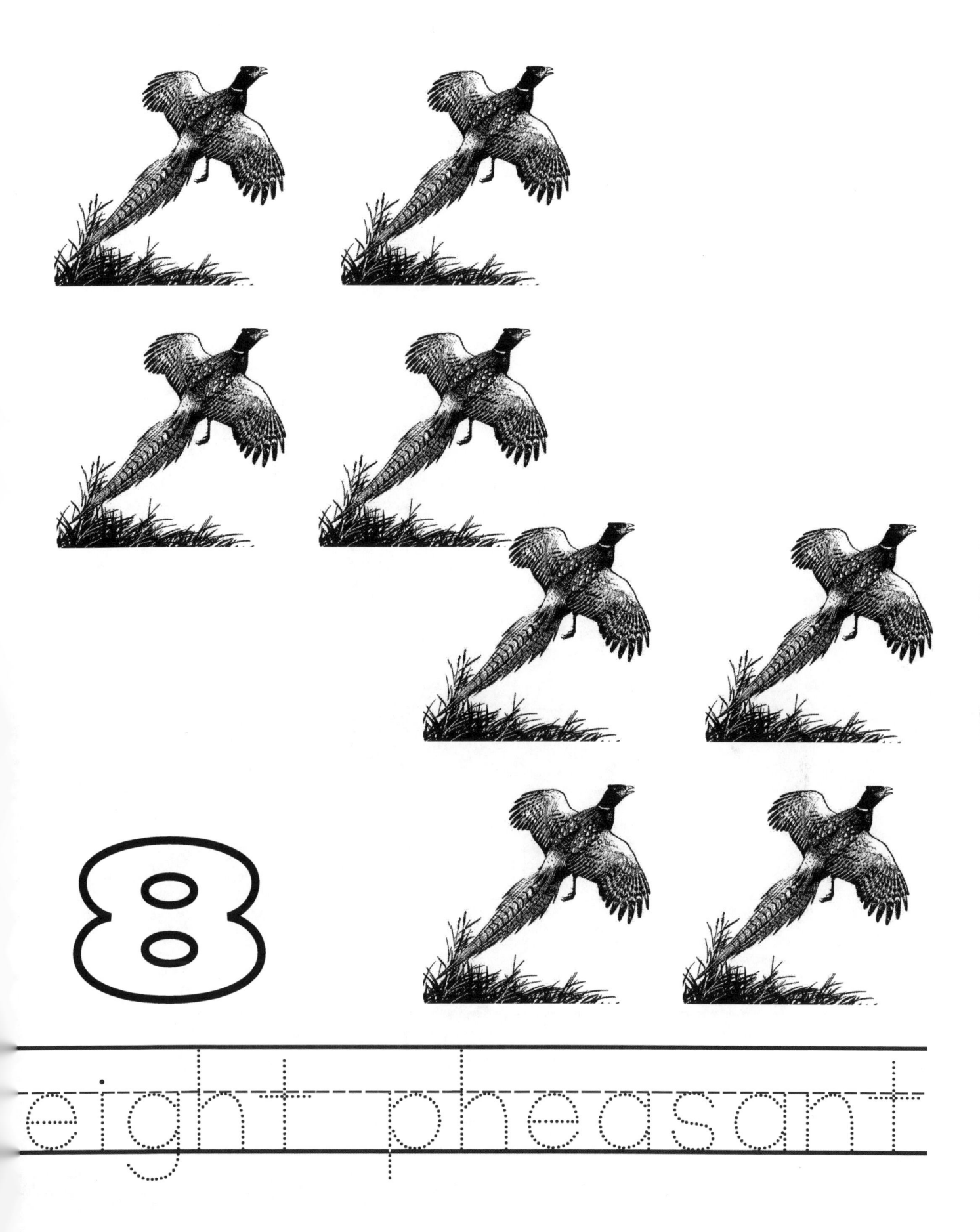

eight pheasant

9

nine deer

10
Dogs

Elements included from Ringneck Ranch, LLC

Learn more at:
www.RingneckRanch.net

Thank you for supporting our small family business!

Learn more at:

www.WyomingisHome.com

Questions or suggestions for improvement?

Rianna@LittleRedHills.com

Wholesale order questions for your shop?

Rianna@LittleRedHills.com

Made in the USA
Las Vegas, NV
07 October 2024

96380645R00024